IT'S TIME TO EAT MAMONCILLOS

It's Time to Eat MAMONCILLOS

Walter the Educator

Silent King Books
A WhichHead Entertainment Imprint

Disclaimer

This book is a literary work; the story is not about specific persons, locations, situations, and/or circumstances unless mentioned in a historical context. Any resemblance to real persons, locations, situations, and/or circumstances is coincidental. This book is for entertainment and informational purposes only. The author and publisher offer this information without warranties expressed or implied. No matter the grounds, neither the author nor the publisher will be accountable for any losses, injuries, or other damages caused by the reader's use of this book. The use of this book acknowledges an understanding and acceptance of this disclaimer.

It's Time to Eat MAMONCILLOS is a collectible early learning book by Walter the Educator suitable for all ages belonging to Walter the Educator's Time to Eat Book Series. Collect more books at WaltertheEducator.com

USE THE EXTRA SPACE TO TAKE NOTES AND DOCUMENT YOUR MEMORIES

MAMONCILLOS

It's time to eat, come gather near,

It's Time to Eat
Mamoncillos

The mamoncillo fruit is here!

Round and green, so small and bright,

A treat to bring us pure delight.

We crack the shell, just give a press,

Inside's a treasure, I must confess.

A juicy pulp, so orange and sweet,

The mamoncillo's such a treat!

It grows on trees so tall and high,

Reaching up into the sky.

From sunny lands where breezes flow,

It's nature's gift to help us grow!

Take a bite and let it play,

The tangy taste will make your day.

A little sweet, a little sour,

This fruit is packed with nature's power!

It's Time to Eat
Mamoncillos

Roll it gently in your mouth,

Taste the flavors heading south.

It's smooth and fun, a snack so fine,

A treat from nature's special vine.

Its seed is big, but don't you frown,

Just nibble the pulp all around.

Spit the seed out when you're done,

Eating mamoncillo is so much fun!

It's healthy too, so full of zest,

Vitamin-packed, it's one of the best.

It helps us play, it helps us grow,

It's the perfect fruit, as we all know.

Share with friends, pass it around,

The joy of fruit can soon be found.

Mamoncillo brings us cheer,

It's Time to Eat
Mamoncillos

A tasty snack when friends are near.

So small and green, a little ball,

But it's the best snack of them all.

One by one, we eat with glee,

This special fruit's for you and me.

So when it's time for something new,

Remember mamoncillo too!

Crack, nibble, share, and play,

It's Time to Eat
Mamoncillos

The perfect fruit for any day!

ABOUT THE CREATOR

Walter the Educator is one of the pseudonyms for Walter Anderson. Formally educated in Chemistry, Business, and Education, he is an educator, an author, a diverse entrepreneur, and he is the son of a disabled war veteran. "Walter the Educator" shares his time between educating and creating. He holds interests and owns several creative projects that entertain, enlighten, enhance, and educate, hoping to inspire and motivate you. Follow, find new works, and stay up to date with Walter the Educator™

at WaltertheEducator.com